THE CAT SCROLLS

A STRATEGIC INNER JOURNEY; BUILD YOUR INNER WORLD and BECOME THE BEST YOU

NAOKO OSHIMA

Balboa Press books may be ordered through booksellers or by contacting:

Balboa Press
A Division of Hay House
1663 Liberty Drive
Bloomington, IN 47403
www.balboapress.com
844-682-1282

ISBN: 979-8-7652-3461-7 (sc)
ISBN: 979-8-7652-3462-4 (e)

Library of Congress Control Number: 2022917087

Print information available on the last page.

Balboa Press rev. date: 10/19/2022

BALBOA.PRESS
A DIVISION OF HAY HOUSE

THE CAT SCROLLS

A STRATEGIC INNER JOURNEY; BUILD YOUR INNER
WORLD AND BECOME THE BEST YOU

We want to be happy **inside**

inside? I'm happy when my stomach is full.

Not that kind of happy!

Just kidding...

inner peace... deeper meaning... nirvana... it's all inside.

Don't get me wrong. We need food and shelter but that's only the beginning.

The question is what you want to do with your life.

What kind of person you want to be.

happy inside...
What's it like for you?

There's something...
some kind of opening
inside me.

It opens to
a higher dimension of

ENDLESS possibilities

inspiration, creativity
and everything magical
flow freely for me.

this reality is
so much more
POWERFUL than
the physical world.

it's my
true home!

4

Our beautiful house is only temporary.

Are we getting evicted soon?

Relax.

I'm just telling you

that...

everything we can

see
hear
smell
catch
eat

is temporary.

I'm Aso
I'm fast like an arrow.

I'm Bo.
I meditate everyday
like a Japanese monk.
Bo is a Japanese word for monk.

It's not because
she's bowlegged.

my legs are straight!

Are we sisters?

No, we were strays.

But... we could be
sisters. we just don't know it.   Ok whatever...

I also practice
my own moves
when Bo is busy
meditating.

It's so difficult.
I need to practice hard
everyday and that's
exactly why I love it!

it feels like I'm
flying effortlessly
I'm completely free!
There's this
DEEP SATISFACTION
I can't get
any
other
way.

But...
I get discouraged
when nothing works for some reason
no matter how hard I try...
and this happens frequently.
It feels
I'm wasting time...
goofing off...
I start to believe
something is wrong with me...

trigger point release

pest control

baby sitting

my specialty is internal fitness.

The inner world is like a baby. It needs to be fed, loved, nurtured and trained otherwise it remains helpless.

I worked all sorts of jobs.
I was searching for my life's purpose. Following my gut and heart I found it!!
my passion is to help people find their own paths to fulfillment

It's endless!

I need a new way . . .

I really want to change . . . .

fighting messes up my hair too . . . .

feeling better is power!

Reacting comes from our built-in survival system but you don't need to be ruled by it. you can consciously work around.

PAY ATTENTION

NOTICE when you are about to pounce

oh . . . like . . . catching a thief in the act!

That turns off the default setting. you are free to THINK in any way that gives you a little relief.

Oops... another reacting...

But you felt a little better, right?

I did! So I'm headed in the right direction?

Yup! feelings mirror your inner weather.

It's a cool feedback system available 24/7 for you to make tactical maneuvering so that you can stay focused and grounded.

The opposite of reacting!

PAYING ATTENTION is the beginning of exiting the default.

From there you blaze your path.

You can override your own biological hard-wiring.

Life is too short living by some automatic functions and walking around completely unaware of them.

OK I'm going to
work out right now.
today's program is

RUN!

100 meter all out
10 rounds!
super challenge!

22

I can't
ignore
—that
inside
the house!

ignoring bad stuff... sounds like doing nothing to resolve problems.

It does... what I meant was "Do not get hung up on it"

Work to do... is inside.

Work on what is in your power.

Look beyond what is right in front.

Get a wider deeper point of view.

Transcend. Rise above.

I didn't realize I was beating up myself all the time.

I can start being nice to myself.

No more judging! When I accept and honor everything about me including all my shortcomings there is nothing to fight against!

It's so liberating to notice my own bad habits that kept me stuck.

We are capable of change.

Is knowledge another powerful tool?

Knowledge is limited imagination is more important.

Welcome to
Cosmic Association of
Internal fitness!
I'm Emily
from Meditation Division

aro, did you know...
you already have tasted
the effect of meditation?

When you are in the zone
you are calm and relaxed
but also intensely focused
your ordinary sense of time disappears
your busy thinking mind goes to sleep
you forget all your problems
you are transported to
a higher place

meditation
is another way
    to turn off
    the monkey mind
and
get
    in
        the
            Zone . . . although that's not a goal to seek obsessively
                    meditation is about so much more!
                        what it does for you ripples
                            far and
                                beyond

It
enables
you to explore
more skillful ways to live
no more drifting, just getting by,
leaving life to whims
feeling empty in the heart

The monkey mind is doing
its job of protecting you and
making you functional
in the physical world

Be thankful and
learn to gently move it aside
The calm and peace
blocked behind
can be revealed

That's your true nature, true self
It's always blended with the universe
It's free of the limitations
of the physical
world

41

Thoughts and feelings can communicate to the invisible world of endless possibilities but....

many of us believe those are something we can hide most easily.

That's why we lie and pretend all the time not only to others but also to ourselves we dismiss it like it doesn't exist.

We tend to write off what is intangible, unknown just because we don't know what to do with it.

Always choose to feel good or better than whatever you're feeling when you're down. It's how you stay connected to your true self.

The next step... clearly project your dreams and desires on your inner screen.

Your dreams will come true because your inside is powerful.

Don't think about how on earth it's possible.

Your job is to grow your consciousness big enough so that... your awareness reaches beyond the physical. Then you will find yourself trust the unknown, look forward to it, welcome it, get excited about it.

44

Absolutely!
Fill it with
something
completely new
like a fountain of
exciting fresh ideas,
beautiful images,
heart stopping epiphanies,
super sharp gut feeling, etc

flowing
freely all the time.

How to do that?
Add more
variety
to your inner activities.

Do things that make you go outside logic and reason

45

Thinking in words is not the only way to think.

Thinking beyond words opens the door to different types of inner processing that you can't explain in words.

Practice observing without looking for words to describe no labelling, no judging.

A whole bunch of nonverbal functions will develop which leads to...
sharper intuition
more aha moments
loss of fear etc.

With nonlinear "thinking" you can directly work with your heart and gut, not just the head.

Your conscious mind grows and evolves multidimensionally.

For more, come to my workshop!

47

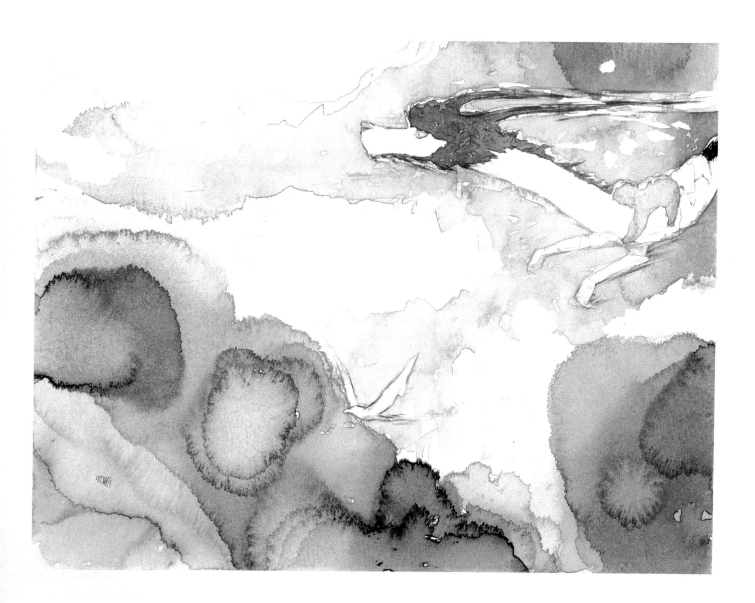

Is this place real?

Of course it is.
   This is our home!

Did you know Bo is
   a new trainer?

I couldn't invite you
   here myself, Aro...
I don't have the power yet.
I'm still a trainer in training.

Doesn't matter. you're here now!

   I'm so excited!

52

I'm madeleine. My kanji name is 恋鈴犬. I grew up in Japan. The only antidote to suffering is to expand your conscious mind... can you give me an example?

Think of suffering as something normal like.....rain.

I wouldn't mind bad weather. When you don't judge it as something to run away from...

It's not an issue any more...

You can finally get to the real issue!

Make your inside bigger and more beautiful than the outer world.

Keep asking yourself questions

What do you want for your life?

What can you do to be better you than yesterday?

Be healthy and fit too!

HOW DO YOU EXPAND CONSCIOUSNESS?

Outside the monkey mind is infinite like the universe.
Use that part and your conscious mind will grow.
Follow your passion, help others, meditate,
excercise, be curious, ask questions,
observe, experiment, try new things,
think for yourself . . . .

and oh!
Track your inner weather at all times.
observe, acknowledge, accept.
Don't demonize negative feelings.
Just choose not to dwell on it too long.
choose a new thought.
feel better.

ALL THOSE THINGS COME FROM YOUR
CONSCIOUS CHOOSING AND CREATING,
NOT FROM THE MONKEY MIND!
YOU'RE BRILLIANT, LUJET!

Thanks, Katrine!
What was your kanji name
madeleine picked
for you?

吠取犬

I love it!

"KNOWLEDGE IS LIMITED"... "KNOWLEDGE IS POWER" WHAT'S GOING ON?

You're manicotti, right? We met before. Knowledge gives you a vantage point but beyond the horizon there's more like this intuition imagination creativity inspiration

these are outside the scope of knowledge.

ALSO THERE'S NO POINT IF YOU DON'T DO ANYTHING WITH IT, RIGHT?

JUST SIT HERE, SIGHTSEEING?

That's kind of nice, but... something may tickle you one day... and you want to get up, do something for some reason...

OUTSIDE THE SCOPE OF KNOWLEDGE!

57

my dream is to turn my passion into a career but... gymnastics...

You think you'll be screwed if you can't make it, don't you?

You can't assume what's in your future based on what you know now. There're way too many surprises and new inspirations that change you and so many other things.

So just forget it?

Quietly

Post it in the background as a friendly reminder while you practice

quiet... background... friendly... no imposition no pressure!

You don't want to stick it in your face!

59

Physical training is not only for the body. It's also for the mind. That's your division, right?

aro, you just made a perfect course description!

When you exercise you can also train your mind at the same time because the body and the mind always work together and evolve together.

Pay attention 100% to how you feel during your workout. Simply calmly observe the whole thing. Control your breathing. Don't listen to your thinking brain complaining, judging, ruining your workout.

60

The body teaches you what other things can't.

It teaches something
so empowering, uplifting,
supersonic, extraterrestrial
and telepathic.

Being in a highly trained body is like
living in the most spiritual cave
in the most beautiful mountain.

You grow a brand new type of consciousness
that is outside the jurisdiction of logic and reason.
You can perceive beyond
what your body can sense.
Your consciousness goes
far and beyond
the
ordinary.

It's like you have an entire galaxy inside expanding everyday.

That's your own homegrown DIY 100% organic genuine Personal power.

The only power you can count on!

Every time you work out hard your comfort zone increases.

That's when your Perception changes!

The body adapts. You become more capable and confident.

Pushing the envelope awakens your hidden abilities.

You discover more of yourself.

Nothing compares to the deep and lasting satisfaction of it.

It permeates to nourish all aspects of your life.

I meditate everyday but my mind still wanders. am I doing it right?

There are results you look for... and... there are also results you don't expect.

I used to hate doing dishes but not any more. I think the change came from my meditation.

So do I, Julian. meditation is a way of opening up. Even if thoughts still keep popping up you are unknowingly moving your border out a little further everyday.

The results are........ always surprising!

you just overhauled what I thought was my goal!

Between black and white lives endless shades of grey.

Oh! another surprise... I can slow down a little now.

welcome to my party!

63

for example...

"my life is good. I have everything I need but deep inside there's this hole asking me to fill...How can I do that?"

"my life is a mess! It feels like I'm living all by myself at the edge of a cliff that could crumble at any moment. What can I do?"

We love our Q & A. We'll be devastated if it ends.

It doesn't end because

questions make inner journey possible.

Personal transformation always starts with a question.

NO QUESTIONS NO JOURNEY

Gol, why are you so small?

Platano did it but I liked it so I'm keeping it for now.

WHY IS IT SO HARD
TO CHANGE?
WE ALL WANT TO
CHANGE BAD HABITS...

we naturally, unconsciously
cling to what is familiar & predictable
so that we feel safe & in control.
the biological makeup story again.

OH BOY...

Good news, Manicotti...is
inspiration
has nothing to do with it!

When you are inspired,
you see possibilities more than problems.
Your inside is filled with so much energy.
You can trust the unknown.
You become unshakable.
Every action you take is
joyful in a way...that...
challenges are not intimidating.
failure doesn't discourage you.

"I SHOULD..." TURNS INTO... "I WANT!!"
YOU WILL WANT TO CHANGE!!

Can you share one of your simple tecniques you use all the time?

When things are clearly frustrating I ask myself "Do I need to get frustrated?" my answer is always "no".

To keep my energy alive and well I don't get caught up in that game. Then, great ideas and solutions fly into me!

In being frustrated... you become your own roadblock!

frustration... proves that you are attached to certain outcomes.

It couldn't be simpler than that!

Staying frustrated you are actually shooting yourself in the foot!

... while the real enemy is your own self-limiting thoughts!

asking yourself questions is the countermeasure!

What is your division, Bo?

I don't know.
I'm not specialized yet.

So it's "all-purpose"
for now?

I like that! That's it!
Thanks, platano!

It's catchy too!

You nailed it, Platano!

Bo, you helped me
come this far.
You're awesome!

Thanks, Aro!
You're fun
to work with.

I love helping people
see things themselves
and...wake up from their
self limiting ways.
I love seeing them get inspired.

It makes me feel most alive.
Helping others... also helps me.

I thought inner journey would be
lonely but it's not.

It made me Realize...deep inside
We are all connected.

69

70

EPILOGUE

I call myself a professional introvert because that's what I do better than anything. I'm always drawn to things that make me go within, and I love to dig deep with great curiosity.

Beside painting and exercising I also love to read with my notebook next to me to jot down anything that lights up for me. Art and fitness have been my primary modes of transportation through my inner journey although I didn't pick them out like registering for a college course, it was more like they invited me in as I was drawn to them.

"What is your life all about?" is one of the most profound questions to ask yourself, and thankfully I can now answer that without any hesitation. My life is all about constantly evolving my conscious mind by always following my heart and gut so that I can become more capable, resilient, wiser, kinder, and all-around a better person than before. It's about becoming more by cultivating my personal power, and it's the only power in this world that I have total control over.

After decades of exploration, my inner reality expanded astronomically and my perception was completely changed. A whole new world was constructed within, one filled with infinite possibilities, compassion, and beauty. This reality became a foundation for me; my primary residence with no mailing address. The chaos and impermanence of external reality no longer dictated my life. The physical world in which we all live became only a portion of my reality without losing my ability to function in it. It's the opposite of numbing and escaping from that world through addictions that only leads to self-destruction.

This experience was so incredible that I couldn't help but express it in my work so that I could share it with as many people as possible. If my book inspires others to find their true self, I can loudly say, "I did my job!"

Making of the Book:

When you're an inner explorer by nature, the tendency is to head straight for the self development section every time you walk in a book store or library, and that's always been the case with me. About eight years ago a desire to create my own rendition was born. I foresaw a book filled with uplifting images woven with handwritten words for people leaning toward introspection, searching for meaning and purpose in their lives. But I had no idea how to create and develop characters or construct a story, and I had to set it aside marked as TOO WILD.

Six years ago, my cat Kiupi was dying of old age. He stopped eating and I knew he just entered the final phase. Nine days passed. I was looking at him lying on the kitchen floor and wondered how much longer he would last. Suddenly an idea flew into me like a meteorite crashing into earth from the upper atmosphere. It was a short, but crystal clear message; MAKE ALL OF THE CHARACTERS ANIMALS. It was a slow motion zoomed close movie scene filled with CG rainbows, stars and music. That was all I needed to get started! ANIMALS! Painting them was already my specialty!

I immediately knew the message was from Kiupi. He wanted to help and work with me in the afterlife. He passed away 2 days later. He lived with me for 17 years and has been working with me from the other side ever since. I'm not talking metaphorically here because this book is the result of my personal efforts and the power of the invisible world melding together.

My book project finally started, and in the beginning I only had two main cat characters and no outline! No outline…, according to the writers code of conduct, is a direct violation and you are immediately disqualified. Even if not, it's as reckless as attempting to climb a mountain you don't know with no map, no water, no food, no preparation whatsoever, hoping it all works out magically.

Standing at the foot of the mountain that I didn't know, it looked utterly impossible for me to climb but for some strange reason I wasn't intimidated at all because I was so excited about the project that all I could see was possibilities. There was a force beyond time and space that was pulling me in then pushing me out into orbit.

When you're inspired, nothing can stop you, and that was exactly what was taking place for me. I started by welcoming anything that came to my mind without worrying. I didn't care about figuring out where things would or could fit into the book.

It was like I was slowly bushwhacking my way through in the woods which worked perfectly for me. Those seemingly random ideas began to organize themselves with cohesion and opened the door for more. After a while more characters showed up out of the blue and the outline started to dawn. After all bushwhacking was always the way of all my creative work and beyond, but working on this book took it to the next level.

The main constant to my mental bushwhacking is to keep my inner state calm and free from resistance. Once I'm completely anchored, there is absolutely no resistance when I say to myself, "I can do this!" What I need next, before diving in with my paint brush, is any strong positive feeling for the primary element in each piece. It could be a certain color combination, composition, a shape of an animal, an expression of an animal or anything. This is crucial; it is everything. Feelings come first! If I try to meticulously plan everything, it will stop the free flowing energy of infinite possibilities. Because of this, I also take extra measures to not become frustrated. If I do, I'll get immediately disconnected from those higher frequencies, like a helicopter suddenly breaks down in midair and free-falls.

Every time I mess up my colors or things don't turn out the way I want, I simply accept it as normal, nothing is failure, everything is a process for me to learn what I need to go forward. Everything in this book is a result of my conscious effort to keep my energy pure and strong by constantly monitoring my feelings. When something clicks, it feels so amazing like a beautiful hummingbird is hovering right in front of me, and all is well. If not, I just pack up my paint box, go outdoors, exercise, meditate, pay bills, or clean my house; anything to make some breathing room. This allows me to try again fresh another day.

Creating something from nothing, then moving forward with it was not new to me, and working on this book definitely reinforced that system. It works as I sit down calmly with a clear intention of creating a certain effect, and then let a pencil move on paper. After a while a strong design usually starts to reveal themselves to me as if I attract what I need, and it's the same with writing. I just start pouring down anything that comes to my mind on paper, even though I know it will be later edited or deleted. When nothing seems to be working, I simply stop – making a conscious effort not to get frustrated – and continue on another day, and eventually, things click.

It's an intricate balancing act between the polar opposites of hammering it out and letting it be. As I power through it, the light turns on initiating a chain reaction, and the energy in the invisible world of endless possibilities starts to communicate with me.

It's a collaboration of my efforts in the physical world and the the power in the higher dimensions that make things happen for me. It could be most accurately described as placing myself in alignment with the energy flow of infinite possibilities by getting myself into a certain state of mind, where I'm relaxed and calm with alertness and confidence. I need to fly above the monkey mind territories because nothing creative can be found in their land.

Watercolor is my primary medium, and in art school I did oil painting for a long time but it turned out to be the process of understanding and skill sharpening that I needed to find my own personal expression. I just love the fluidity, transparency, and luminosity of watercolor, and it naturally synchronizes with my inward introspection so perfectly.

Watercolor can be used in all sorts of ways to create different effects. I mainly let water carry the pigment on paper toward my intended direction loosely, like walking a dog extremely long leashed, allowing it to wander far and wide. It's the water leading me but also I'm the one controlling it by moving the paper around, carefully watching it run and dry, mixing in another color at the right moment, etc.

I'm so blessed to have more than one way to walk my inner path. Painting is obviously a stationary activity and it signals me to do the opposite after a while, like the Yin and Yang energy maintaining the optimal balance for me.

Switching between those two modes also keeps me from becoming myopic or stagnant in either direction. They compliment each other and work synergistically to keep me sharp, fresh and strong.

Physical exercise helps to expand my conscious mind in a unique way; one that's very different from painting. If painting is a wide and straight stairway, exercising is a steeper, spiraling flight of stairs that demands something entirely different from me. It teaches me to pay extra attention to relaxing into it in the middle of exertion by regulating my breathing and observing. Once I settle in to the calm, which requires effort and focus in and of itself I'm walking on the bridge to the other side that is unknown where I find my true potential.

Within us all are caves filled with treasures galore, and the only way to discover them is to actually crawl around in the dark. Personally, there is nothing more exciting than finding out something about myself that I never knew before, capabilities and qualities that I would have never known had I just always sat around doing nothing and avoiding difficulties.

In total, it took me six years to finish this book. Each page that made its way into the final copy was one of many "takes." On average, there were three to ten or even more takes for each page with only one exception. If a page didn't feel right to me, I tried again and again until it feels right. I have illustrated for picture books before and I gained so much confidence and skills in my art. But looking back now, it was just warm-up in comparison to this project. Creating both the images and the words added new challenges. Thanks to being fueled by the inexhaustible creative energies from all of the higher dimensions, I didn't get overwhelmed at all. Choosing to keep my inner states balanced enabled me to face the new challenges with joy.

This book was the most outrageous work I have ever done and it changed my life like I just came back from a six year camping and mountain climbing around the entire country. It made me a better artist, trainer, and person as a whole. As my galactic world is ever-expanding, it has proven to me that the combination of inspiration and passion is the strongest driving force of life that can convert obstacles into opportunities, and take you to the epicenter of your own truth. Discovering your life's path and how to walk it isn't difficult if you constantly ask yourself questions, think independently, and listen to your inner callings. Life has so much to offer if you pay attention and start to observe. We all have a choice. We can choose to do the work that can transform our lives or to remain powerless and give up our power to the circumstances.

Backstage Stories:

This book contains practical tools and techniques for personal development like a manual or guide. When I added some flavor of ancient texts written on scrolls like the Dead Sea Scrolls, there was The Cat Scrolls, a new breed of self help book. I thought it would be fun and a little tongue and cheek to think back in time when the entire world was busy with ever-advancing technologies to the point where there was too much of it and it began to disconnect us not only from each other but also from ourselves.

In ancient China there were a series of scrolls written about the strategy and techniques of war. Each chapter was given a different animal nickname. In present day Japan the "The Tiger Scrolls" has become slang for a cheat sheet or secret manual. Here is an example of the original kanji: 虎の巻.

I interjected a few kanji names throughout the book just for fun because I take fun seriously! It's heartwarming and that's power. I'm open to anything that increases my personal power, remember?

The Cat Scrolls has nothing to do with war, but the essence is preserved in the names of the two main characters: Bo and Aro - bow and arrow. Although Bo came from a Japanese word for monk, it had a double meaning – bow and monk. The title "The Cat Scrolls" by itself didn't entirely explain what the book was about and needed a subtitle. I gravitated to the word "build" because that's exactly what it felt like to me when I looked back on my own inner journey. It always reminded me of the adage "Rome wasn't built in a day." I actually built another colossal world inside that was so much better than Rome where people killed each other like it was business as usual.

Special Thanks

Akiko Sato, my sister sometimes uses words and phrases that make me pause and think as I notice there is something inside me stirring up, and it smells yummy. I once sent her, via email, some excerpts from a book I recently read. She emailed me back, "So cool! It's going to be included in my Tiger Scrolls." A certain part of my brain was activated, and it was in that moment that the title of this book, The Cat Scrolls was born. Even if I had toiled for hours and days trying to find a decent title, I would never have come up with something so distinctive, original and adventurous like that.

Art Driscoll, my significant other, is always willing to be the devil's advocate. He can play out views and opinions that confront or reject mine, and I learned not to take anything for granted, especially my work in which I could easily get so steadfast. His cool, no nonsense observation delivered with no sugar coating was exactly what I needed to keep me in checks and balances. His lifelong passion for fitness and health forever changed so many people's lives around him for so many years including mine, which became the basis for developing Mo the mountain lion.

Colyn Freundorfer, my trusted editor hardly knew that he would end up being appointed as such when I first asked for his feedback about a particular section of the book. His insights always mirrored back to me what I still needed to work on with extraordinary clarity and precision which prompted me to search even further for fresh, new, and eye opening ideas and words that I would never have reached otherwise. My two month long search for the last part of the subtitle abruptly ended when he ever so casually suggested "Become the Best You."

Sonia Vattier, a great friend from the Art Student League is gifted with an otherworldly life force, sensibility to the finest nuances and aesthetic that I've never seen in anybody. I still remember a little note she left for me 24 years ago, and I couldn't stop looking at it for five minutes because her handwriting was so exotic, eloquent and one of a kind. I loved it so much that I kept it for all these years. She accidentally saved me from auditioning 30 people for the "voice" of Lujet.

Jake Lewis, my former colleague left me a note one day about a client cancellation. His distinctive handwriting blew me away. I've never seen anything so unforgettably bold, gutsy, and crisply legible with masculine thick bones. I secretly started to collect his notes since then. My collection served me perfectly well when Mo the mountain lion suddenly showed up and needed a voice that would match the character.

Kiupi, my cat lived and evolved with me during those 17 years together, and eventually ushered me into this book project. He taught me so many invaluable life lessons, and for the most part he made me laugh everyday and kept my oxytocin level high. Without his telepathic communication with me on August 9th, 2016, you wouldn't be holding this book and reading it now.

Beaver, my cat played herself in the Q & A section. I hope she didn't mind….I couldn't ask her because she moved to the other side two years ago. At least I'm deeply satisfied that she is memorialized in the book forever. Since her character was real it brought life to the book.

Poppy, Art's dog, my "stepdog" became the model for Titan, and he added the variety I needed to the animal crew. Unlike cats, dogs love whatever their humans do with them so I took the liberty. He must be jumping up and down in joy on the other side, and barking happily "I'm in it! I'm in it!"

My special thanks also goes to my parents who always encourage me to do what I love to do, my animals of both sides, animals in nature, nature itself that is always my inspiration, and the creative power of the infinite that is my driving force and guiding light.

And I thank you all for reading my book. I hope you enjoyed it and it filled you with special positive feelings. Inner journey requires nothing; no ticket to buy, no reservation to make, no suitcase to pack, and no need to save money for it. You can start anytime anywhere and I guarantee it will be the best thing you'll ever do for yourself. I'm sure you will come home being the best version that you can be with your Inner Kingdom firmly established forever.

I would love to hear about your inner journey. We can stay connected through my online gallery: www.naokooshima.com